DALMA
RABBIT

DIY * PAPER
SQUISHY
HALLOWEEN

DALMA RABBIT

ISBN: 9798340121035

MATERIALS

YOU NEED

COLORS
Markers, crayons, pencils..

SCISSORS

TAPE
Transparent.

BOX TAPE
Transparent for laminate
your squishy.

STUFFING
You can use cushion or toy
stuffing, bubble wrap, tissue paper,
paper or plastic bags..

TUTORIALS, INSPIRATION AND NEWS.

@dalmarabbit

#dalmarabbit

DALMA
RABBIT

SHARE YOUR
PROJECT

YOUTUBE CHANNEL

 Subscribe and like.

SQUISHIES INSTRUCTIONS

1 Cut page you want coloring.

2 Color design.

3 Coat it with packing tape.

4 Cut along the line.

5 Tape the front and back together along the edges

6 Leave an opening for filling.

7 Stuffing.

8 Seal the opening with adhesive tape.

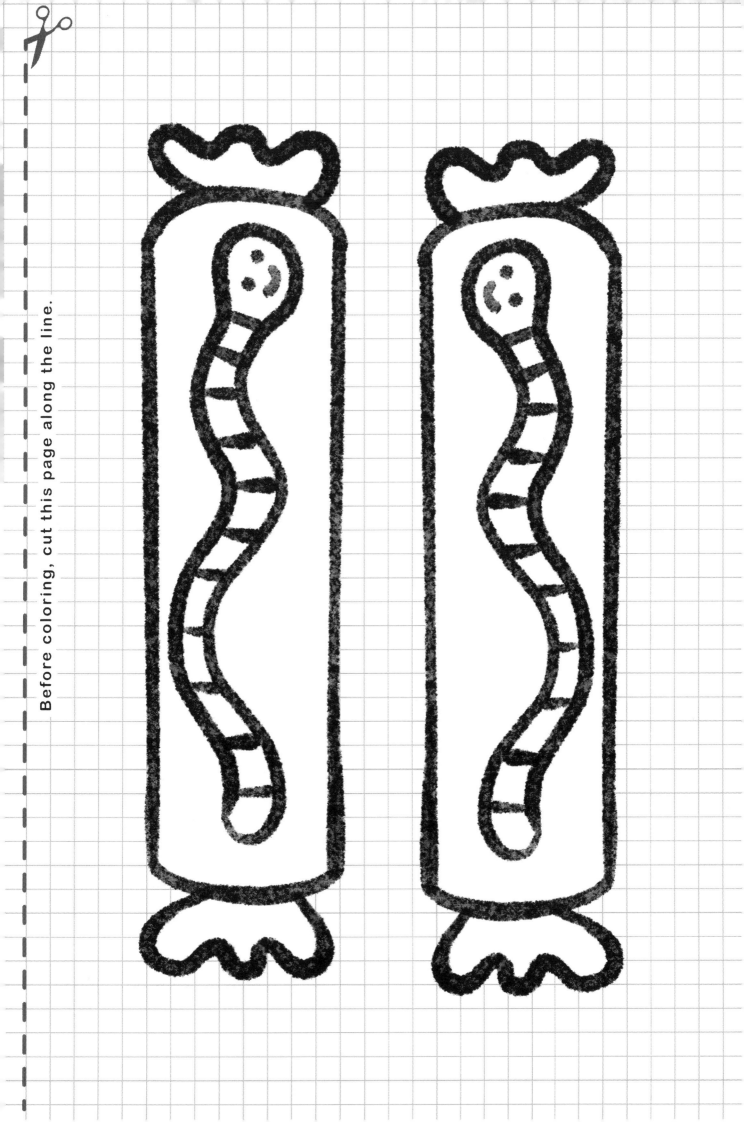

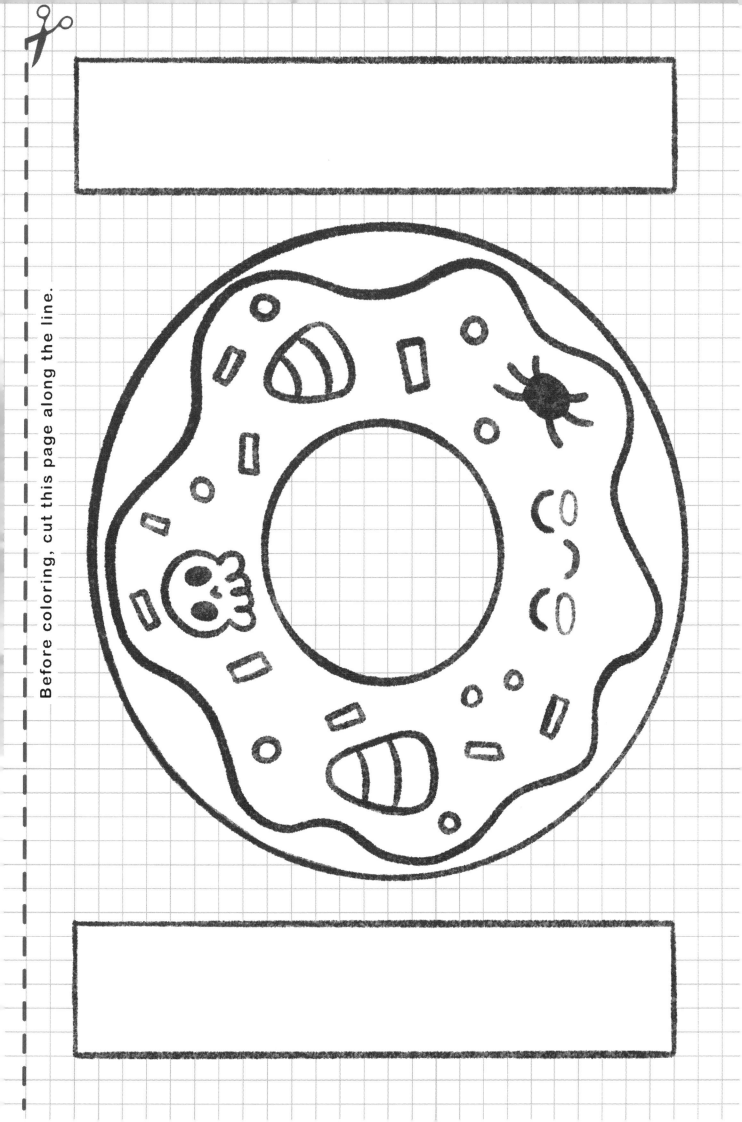

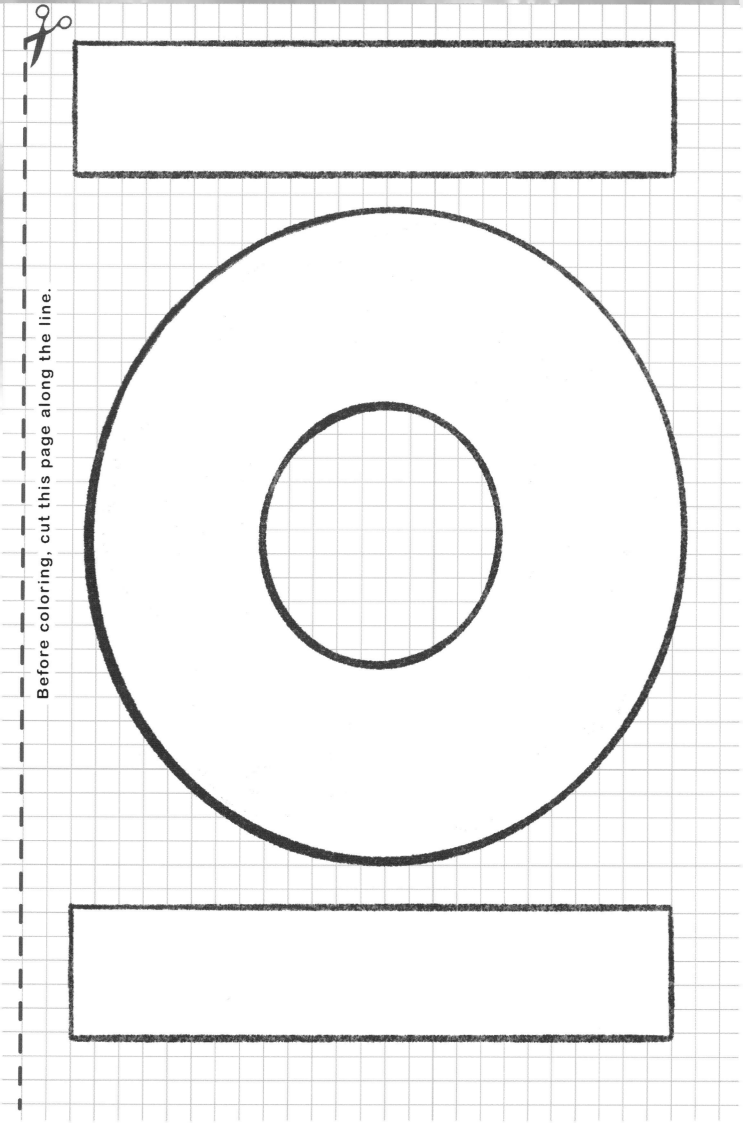

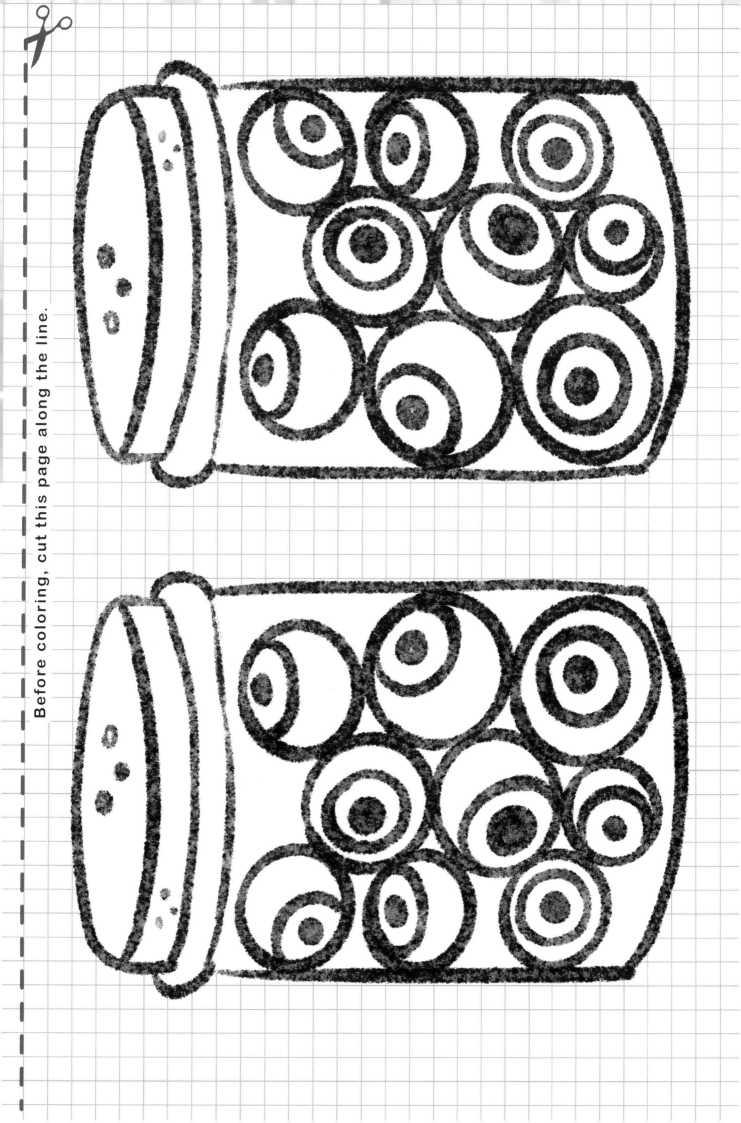

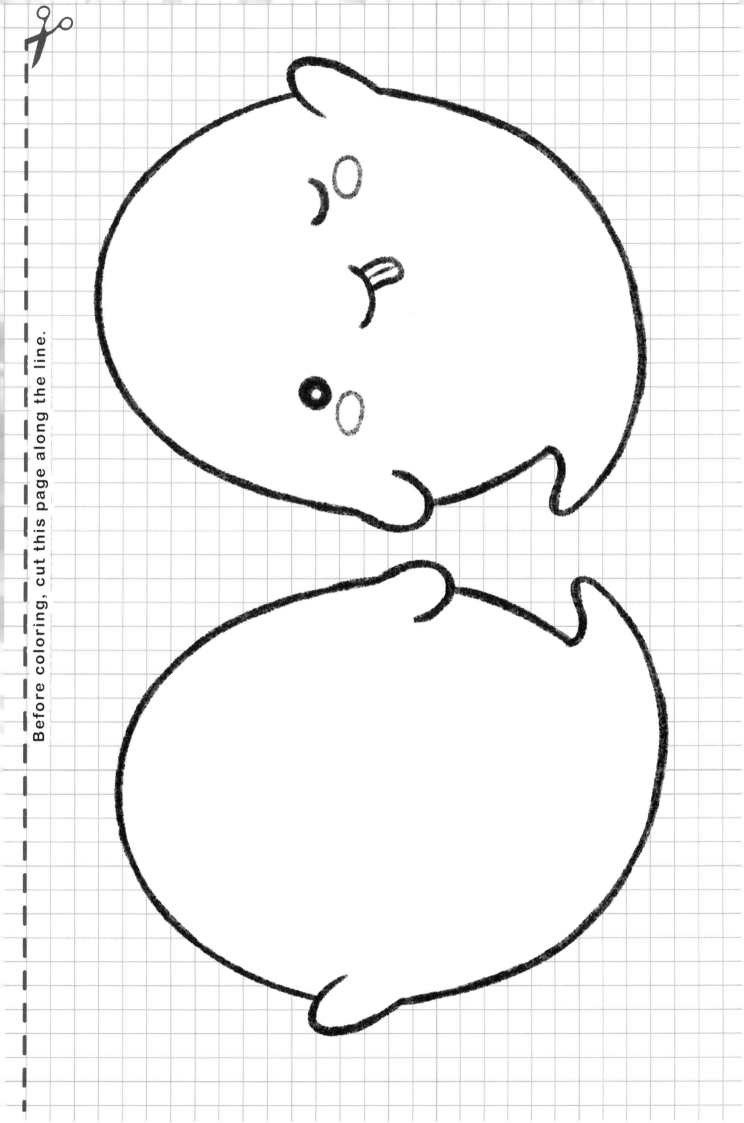

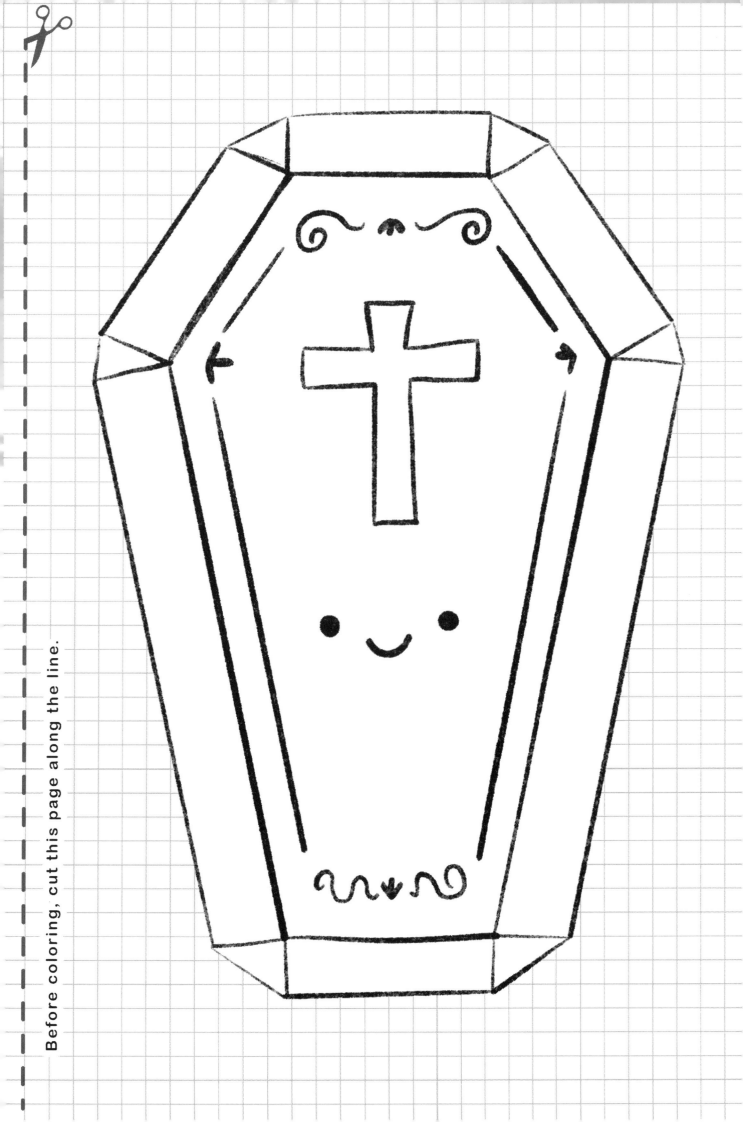

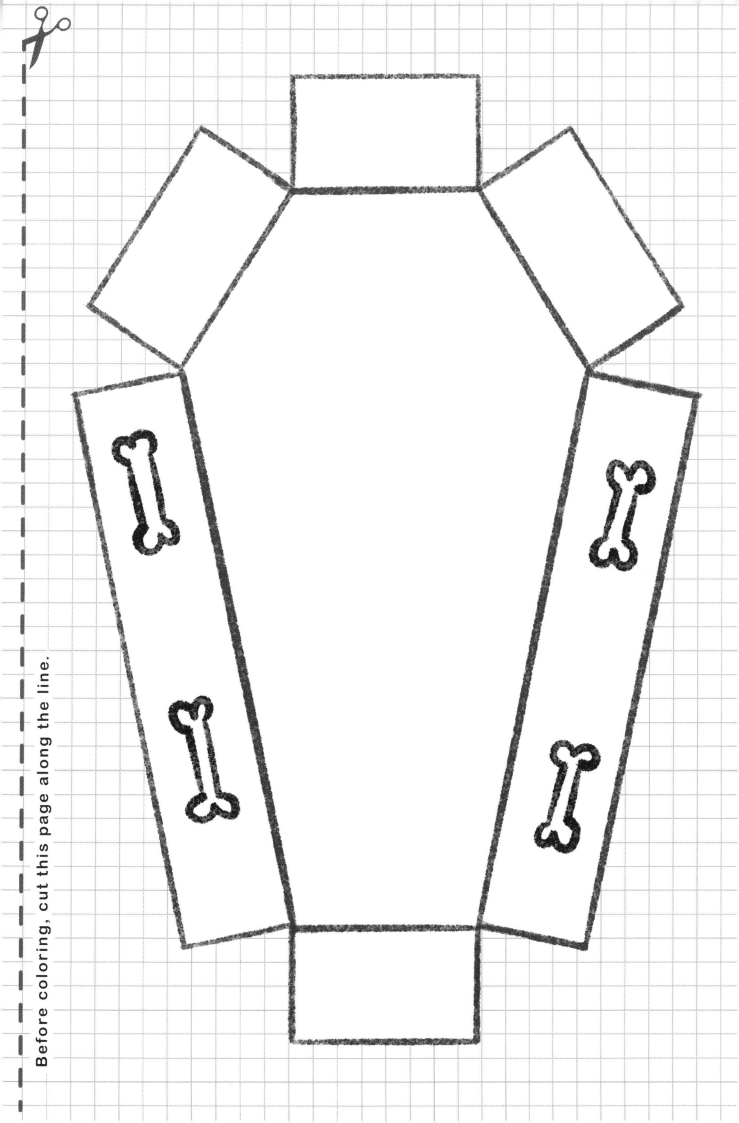

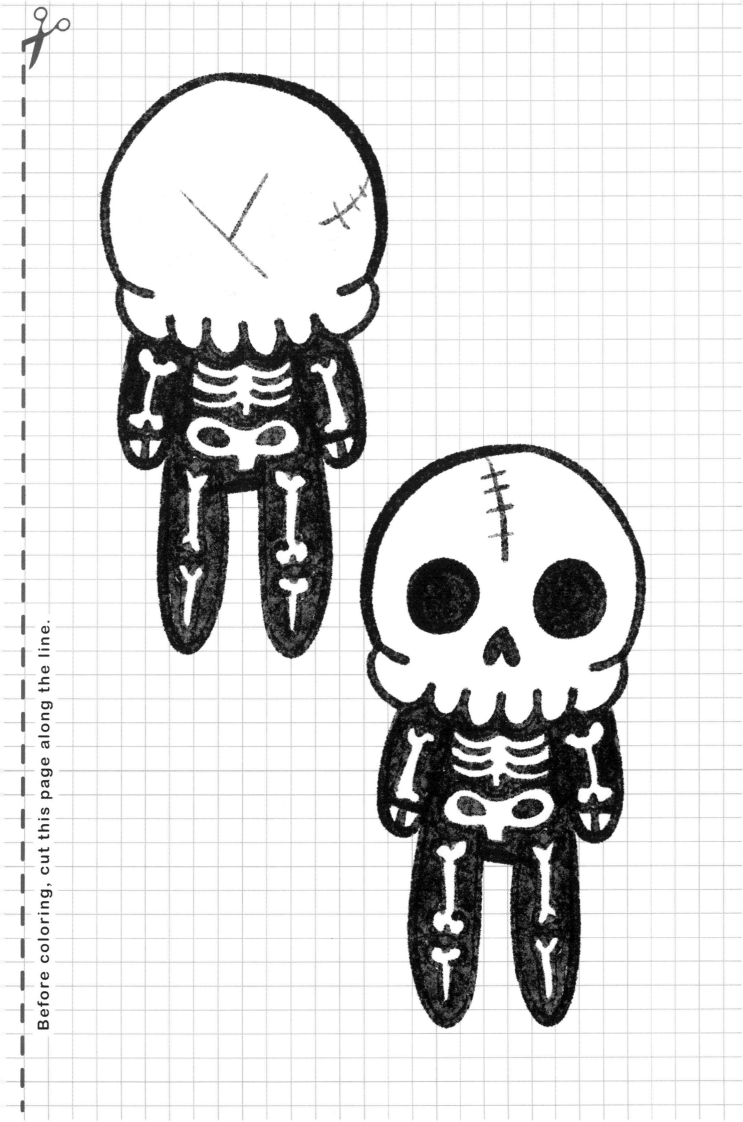

Made in United States
Troutdale, OR
10/29/2024

24274304R00038